odd critters: 2

by Sarah Forrest

No part of this publication may be reproduced without written permission of the publisher, except for use in the classroom.

Printed in the United Kingdom by Ex Why Zed Print.
First Edition, August 2021

ISBN: 978-1-911151-27-2

© Oxford Learning Solutions 2021

All Aboard Learning, 267 Banbury Road, Oxford OX2 7HQ

AllAboardLearning.com

Compatible with All Aboard Phonics Second Edition.

All Aboard Phonics Phase 5 Unit 2 Week 7

Week 7	<a>: /a/ /ay/ /o/ /ar/ /or/
Week 8	<c>: /k/ /s/ <ch>: /ch/ /sh/ /k/
Week 9	<ea>: /ee/ /e/ <ear>: /ear/ /air/ /er/
Week 10	<ey>: /ee/ /ay/ <g>: /g/ /j/
Week 11	<i>: /i/ /igh/ <ie>: /igh/ /ee/
Week 12	<o>: /o/ /oa/ /u/ <oo>: /oo/ /oo(k)/
Week 13	<ou>: /ow/ /oo(k)/ /oo/ /oa/ <ow>: /oa/ /ow/
Week 14	<s>: /s/ /zh/ <th>: "think" vs "that"
Week 15	<u>: /u/ /oo(k)/ /yoo/ <u_e>: /oo/ /yoo/
Week 16	<ue>: /yoo/ /oo/ <y>: /y/ /ee/ /i/ /igh/

All Aboard Phonics decodable books have a carefully controlled vocabulary and are specifically designed for children who are learning to read and write with All Aboard Phonics, or beginner readers learning at home.

The panda ant is not a panda or an ant.

It's a killer wasp!

Its sting is so strong it can kill a cow.

The angora rabbit is a big ball of fur.

If you forget to cut its hair, the hair blocks it from seeing!

When it eats its hair by mistake, the hair blocks up its guts.

A hagfish makes slime to escape tight spots.

It can fill up a bin with slime in the time it takes you to brush teeth!

If slime goes up its nose, the hagfish sneezes it out.

Alpacas hum as a way to chat.

Like a cat, they always poo in the same spot.

So you can have one as a pet!

The glass frog has clear skin.

You can see its bones and guts. Rather cool!

Image Credits:

Photo 1: ID 1294686742 © Dustin Rhoades | Shutterstock.com

Photo 2: ID 1866193417 © javiermartinez22 | Shutterstock.com

Photo 3: ID 45723755 © Mikhail Dudarev | Dreamstime.com

Photo 4: ID 131672389 © Isselee | Dreamstime.com

Photo 5: ID 19572587 © Isselee | Dreamstime.com

Photo 6: ID 131672389 © Isselee | Dreamstime.com

Photo 7: ID 5562913789 © dirtsailor2003 | Flickr.com

Photo 8: ID 69815264 © Ffennema | Dreamstime.com

Photo 9: ID 69815298 © Helena Cadanova | Dreamstime.com

Photo 10: ID 160304005 © Murbanska00 | Dreamstime.com

Photo 11: ID 116087411 © Fotorince | Dreamstime.com

Photo 12: ID 54343701 © Doty911 | Dreamstime.com

Photo 13: ID 14101681 © Dirk Ercken | Dreamstime.com

Photo 14: ID 20415281 © Brandon Alms | Dreamstime.com